Turning Temptations into
TRIUMPHS

God's Proven Strategies
Against Satanic Devices

SAM O. ADEWUNMI

COVENANT PUBLISHING

Turning Temptations into Triumphs
Sam O. Adewunmi

Unless otherwise stated, all scripture quotations are taken from the Holy Bible, New King James Version (NKJV). Other versions cited are NIV, KJV, GNB, God's Word, MSG, LEB and NLT.

ISBN 978-1-907734-13-7
First Edition
First Printing February 2015

For permission requests, write to the publisher, addressed "Attention: Permission Coordinator" at the email address below:

Covenant Publishing
samadewunmi@btinternet.com

Covenant Publishing is part of New Covenant Church
Charity Registered in England & Wales number 1004343
Registered Address: 506-510 Old Kent Road. LONDON SE1 5BA

Cover Design by Covenant Publishing Team
Sam Adewunmi's photo by David Adetoye
Published by Covenant Publishing
Printed in the United Kingdom

TABLE OF CONTENTS

DEDICATION

To God and all who are struggling to resist the temptations of the evil one

FOREWORD

It is without a doubt that God is committed to the success, triumph and freedom of His people as evident in His design, creation and the positioning of humanity on earth. The resources He provides are designed and planned to ensure that humanity, His crowning glory in creation, would reflect Him, in splendour.

However, a college degree is not required to observe and acknowledge that God's original intention is blighted by humanity giving access and a field day to the devil. Instead of freedom, people prefer needless chains. People are bound emotionally, financially, relationally and spiritually. These are invisible chains, but their effects are there to see.

In this book, Turning Temptations into Triumphs, Sam endeavors to bring people to the realisation of God's intention of blessing, humanity's invention of ruin (internally and externally), and God's intervention to bring us back to Himself and live in total triumph. In a very well thought out manner, he makes us see that, it is usually the actions of a few that bring suffering, misery and pain to many. This is clearly supported by the decisions, choices and actions of people like

Introduction

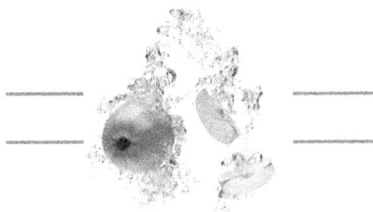

SHOW UP, STEP UP AND STAND UP

Had Adam known what you and I now know, he probably would have given more thought to his action. We know that what we do or omit to do knowing we are supposed to do might end up affecting four generations after us. Such knowledge was not available to Adam. The entire universe is suffering the consequences of Adam's wrong choices.

"For we know that the whole creation groans and labours with birth pangs together until now" (Romans 8:22).

The question that must now be answered is this: What would it take to reverse this catastrophe? The answer is found in Romans 8:19. We need to come out of hiding. We need to show up, step up and stand up. We manifest His power when we stop hiding and begin to establish God's kingdom here on earth.

> *"For the earnest expectation of the creature waiteth for the manifestation of the sons of God" (Romans 8:19, KJV).*

God is looking for a remnant that will not deny Him or deny their faith. Showing up, stepping up and standing up means we would be bold to declare our allegiance to Him. It means we would be proud to be identified with Him. We may take an unpopular stance; however, it is better to stand with the One that matters at the end of the day. This is not only in our Churches. It is not in the apparels we wear or the music we sing, but out on the streets and in the market place.

The world needs to see us. They need to see a generation that is not in the kingdom business for their own benefits. They want to see a place where their children are safe at the hands of their ministers. They are looking for a place where their wives and daughters will not be abused; a place where their sons will not be molested.

The world is waiting for a people that will report to work on time, stay at work and complete their shifts; a people who would not call sick when they are okay and well enough to work; a people that will do beyond the expected, not in a bid to win man's approval but doing so as unto the Lord. When it comes to consistency, their employers are proud of them and when there is redundancy, they are the last to be considered.

The world is waiting for a people that when they say 'I do,' they really do. Not because it is fashionable to say 'I do' but because it comes from the depth of their being; those who would say, 'for better or worse,' and stay put, whether it is better or worse. We are talking about a generation that will look after their wives and their children, not shifting or shirking their responsibilities. The world is already too filled with individuals raised in single parent homes.

The world is waiting to see in us a huge river, gracefully moving in the might of the Holy Spirit – irresistible and unrelenting. Not a bunch of motionless cesspit of religious people or a shallow lake going nowhere, but a monumental river with an inconceivable current. The moment you become part of it, you are no longer your own but entering with reckless abandon, allowing the current of God to carry you to wherever He wishes.

The world is waiting to see a church that is not only physically growing but also a church that is holy and blameless, without spot or wrinkle. They are waiting for the manifestation of a church that is after the Lord's heart where race and gender differences are what make it whole and not what brings division. A church where every soul is significant; though the salvations of its individual souls are personal, the community is essentially one.

The world is tired of hypocrites; who says one thing but practice another. In the public, they are the nicest of people, but privately, they terrorise their families. They tell their children 'not-to' but do the 'not-to'; leaving them more confused. They wear nice clothes on Sunday but you cannot even recognise them as Christians on Monday through Saturday. In their closets, they watch immoral stuffs and read immoral junks.

People want to see those whose 'yes is yes', and 'no is no.' They are no longer interested in rhetoric but want to know what is on our minds even if it is at variance with their interests. Least, they can make up their mind if they want to join our camps. The time of pretence and lies are over. God is looking for a generation whose words can be counted on; on whose promises we can rely.

Until we show up, stand up and step up, we would continually be the laughing stock of a perishing world. Until we stop blaming the devil for our actions; giving him some recognition and taking responsibility for our mistakes, the church would not be taken serious.

The sacrifices may be high but the rewards are higher. Your friends may be doing it but you have to refuse to join in. And, if you stick with it, you shall surely rejoice. It may be popular to cheat but you prefer rather to go without; that is sacrifice and it shall not go unnoticed and unrewarded. After all, the bible says, you shall be perfect, established, strengthened and settled for your sacrifice. That's the promise of God.

> *"But may the God of all grace, who called us to His eternal glory by Christ Jesus, after you have suffered a while, perfect, establish, strengthen, and settle you" (1 Peter 5:10).*

It was tempting for Jesus to quit, yet He did not. It was easy to let go, but He refused. What did He do? He endure the pain, the agony, and the shame of the cross all because of us and the reward waiting to be claimed.

"Therefore, since we are surrounded by such a huge crowd of witnesses to the life of faith, let us strip off every weight that slows us down, especially the sin that so easily trips us up. And let us run with endurance the race God has set before us. We do this by keeping our eyes on Jesus, the champion who initiates and perfects our faith. Because of the joy awaiting him, He endured the cross, disregarding its shame. Now He is seated in the place of honor beside God's throne" (Hebrews 12:1-2, NLT).

It was worth it at the end. What would you have done? Say it loud and let the Lord hear you and let your neighbour be your witness.

In humility, I invite you to join me in declaring that it can be done. We can be faithful husbands, honest employees, disciplined disciples, trusted leaders, enviable dads, and good stewards. Oh yes we can!

The devil can be defeated. He can be beaten, squashed, and shamed. You can stand your ground and say 'No' to the devil and 'Yes' to God. Oh yes you can! It's not going to be a walk in the park but you would get there.

Welcome to freedom living. The journey starts here; I mean, on the next page.

Chapter One

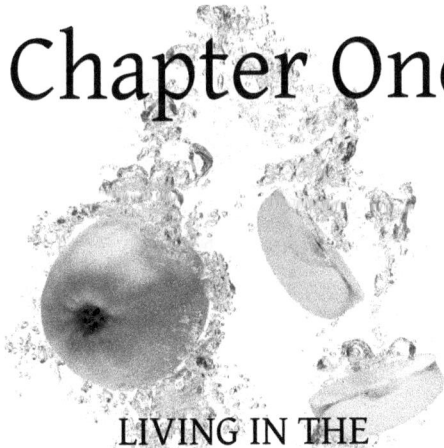

LIVING IN THE
FEAR OF GOD

Chapter One

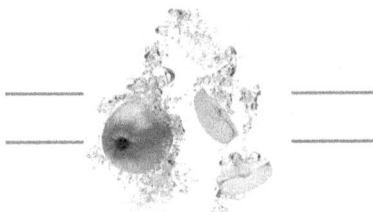

LIVING IN THE FEAR OF GOD

We celebrated the 200th year of the abolition of slavery in 2007 which related to physical liberation. Although slave trading is now illegal, and people may no longer be physically enslaved, they can be taken captive by so many other things. For example people may be incarcerated by debt.

"Poor people are slaves of the rich. Borrow money and you are the lender's slave" (Proverbs 22:7, GNB).

Many people have gone into debt and because of that, they have become slaves to the lender. Until they have fully paid whatever was taken as loan, they will continue to work for the lender. It is very crucial that we do not get into debt so that we can fulfill God's plan for our lives without anything holding us back.

Although our physical and material lives are important, the most important area of life Christians have to seek deliverance and pay more attention is our spiritual lives. If you spend time profitably and do well economically but neglect your spiritual needs, you will eventually lose everything.

> "Will people gain anything if they win the whole world but lose their life? Of course not! There is nothing they can give to regain their life" (Matthew 16:26, GNB).

You can have everything and yet possess nothing. Material success is not the ultimate goal one should seek in life. Spiritual fulfilment approved of God should be everyone's desire. So how can we redress ungodly desires? How can we refocus our gaze? How can this be done?

Living in the fear of the Lord will help us to avoid selling our future to the devil. Making sound moral judgement and choices will help us to avoid heartaches like those of Adam, Abraham and David. Our decisions will either make or mar your future. If we want a triumphant finish, we have to work on your moral choices.

People do not have to be in chains to be bound but can be in chains and yet are free. Not everyone in prison is bound, and not everyone on our streets is free. One may be physically free but emotionally, mentally, financially and morally bound.

Mr. Spurgeon once made a parable. He said, "There was once a tyrant who summoned one of his subjects into his presence, and ordered him to make a chain. The poor blacksmith – that was his occupation – had to go to work and forge the chain. When it was done, he brought it into the presence of the tyrant and was ordered to take it away and make it twice the length. He brought it again to the tyrant, and again he was ordered to double it. Back he came when he had obeyed the order, and the tyrant looked at it, and then commanded the servants to bind the man hand and foot with the chain he had made and cast him into prison.

"That is what the devil does with men," Mr. Spurgeon said. "He makes them forge their chain, and then binds them hand and foot with it, and casts them into outer darkness."

Friends, this is just what the drunkard, gambler, blasphemer, and every sinner is doing. Thank God, we can tell them of a deliverer. The Son of God has the power to break every one of their fetters if they will only come to Him[1].

I have counselled many believers who are addicts of pornography, lies, alcohol, or drugs of every kind. They are free but still bound. It is possible as a child of God to be held captive by the devil in particular areas. Many Christians refuse to admit that they are struggling with pornography, drinking or gambling addictions. Others are held captive by debt, immigration problems, failures and other limitations placed on them by choice or other people's negligence.

Many people quote what they do not fully understand. Here is a scripture commonly used.

"If the Son therefore shall make you free, you are free indeed" (John 8:36, KJV).

Free from what? The answer is simple yet profound: free from the guilt, presence and penalty of sin but not the power of sin. I know this is hard to swallow. The text is talking about the first level of freedom, nothing more. Jesus was talking about Justification not sanctification. Justification sets you free from the guilt, presence and penalty of sin, but only Sanctification can set you free from the power of sin and that is the work of the Holy Spirit after conversion. Many are free from the presence of sin but not from its power. Even Apostle Paul had this struggle in his life. That was what he said in Romans 7:14-23. He was free from the presence of sin but not its power. He later found a way out through Sanctification.

On one of his European tours, the master magician and locksmith Harry Houdini found himself locked in by his thinking. After he had been searched and manacled in a Scottish town jail, the old turnkey shut him in a cell and walked away. Houdini quickly freed himself from his shackles and then tackled the cell lock. However, despite all his efforts, the lock would not open. Finally, ever more desperate but utterly exhausted, he leaned against the door, and it swung open so unexpectedly that he nearly fell headlong into the corridor. The turnkey had not locked it[2].

The Israelites left Egypt, but Egypt did not leave them. They crossed the Red (Reed) Sea but still had the Jordan to cross. They all perished in the wilderness save two, Joshua and Caleb. They were baptised in Moses but not in Joshua. They were justified but not sanctified. They negotiated their freedom with Pharaoh while they were in Egypt, but there was no one to negotiate with in the wilderness but their hearts. With the army of Pharaoh they conquered but of the battle of the mind they lost. It is in the ministry of the Holy Spirit, through Sanctification, that any solution can be found.

> "'... Not by might nor by power, but by My Spirit,' says the LORD of hosts" (Zechariah 4:6).

Those are free who are in prison, but have Jesus, and those are bound who reside in their home without Jesus. Freedom is not the absence of physical chains; it is the presence of Jesus. Everyone came to the earth, bound. They may appear on the outside to be free but, on the inside, they are bound, and only Jesus sets men free. To be held captive is to be placed under restrictions within a boundary (physical or spiritual) against your will. Paul cried,

> "Oh, what a miserable person I am! Who will free me from this life that is dominated by sin?" (Romans 7:24, NLT).

> "Thank God! The answer is in Jesus Christ our Lord. So you see how it is: In my mind I really want to obey God's law, but because of my sinful nature I am a slave to sin" (Romans 7:25, GNB).

Jesus said of Himself, "... I have come that they may have life (Zoe), and that they may have it more abundantly (perissos)" (John 10:10).

It is two-stage deliverance. *Zoe* is the life of God received at salvation. *Perissos* is the beyond measure life after salvation; the superior, superabundant, excessive life of God. A Christian may have 'zoe' but not 'perissos' because they have been held captive in an area. So Jesus came to proclaim liberty to the captives.

"The Spirit of the Lord God is upon Me, because the LORD has anointed Me... to proclaim liberty to the captives" (Isaiah 61:1).

Slavery to Sin

Writing to Christians in Rome Paul penned this,

"Surely you know that when you surrender yourselves as slaves to obey someone, you are in fact the slaves of the master you obey – either of sin, which results in death, or of obedience, which results in being put right with God" (Romans 6:16, GNB).

Everything we do have consequences. What we are experiencing today are fruits of seeds previously sown and they in turn become seeds that may yield future fruits. If we serve Satan and become a slave to sin, it will lead to death. If we serve God and are His slave unto obedience, it leads to righteousness. That is just the way it goes. Our actions or omissions have their consequences. There is a wage, a payback. If we do not get the results now, wait and it will come. If we do not pay for it now, we may be paid for it. There is always a wage.

> "For the wages of sin is death, but the gift of God is eternal life in Christ Jesus our Lord" (Romans 6:23).

Lots of people have paid the ultimate untimely price for a little indulgence – so to speak. Some have died of AIDS or STIs because they could not control their sexual appetites.

> "Do not be deceived, God is not mocked; for whatever a man sows, that he will also reap. For he who sows to his flesh, will of the flesh reap corruption, but he who sows to the spirit will of the spirit reap everlasting life" (Galatians 6:7-8).

Generational Curses

Those who claim that there is nothing like generational curses lack understanding. It will take several pages to fully explain the ministry of deliverance. But let's do a one-paragraph crash course.

Generational curses are real. Demonic possession occurs in the realm of the spirit while demonic oppression occurs in the realm of the soul and the flesh. For an unsaved person, he or she can be both possessed and oppressed because the pronounced curse of the Old Covenant is active up to the fourth generation of the unsaved. When we become saved, our spirit is renewed but the soul and the flesh are not. Justification deals with the spirit in man but deliverance deals with the soul and flesh. The devil is unable to possess the believer, but he or she can be oppressed. When we cast out demons, we are dealing with the generational consequences of idolatry. As explained earlier, this is two-stage deliverance. Jesus raised Lazarus from the dead, but Lazarus remained bound until the disciples were instructed to lose him. A lot of Christians are alive but may be bound in certain areas of their lives. The rest is for another day.

The effects of sins committed may be felt up to the fourth generation. By one act of disobedience, you could have sold your children, grandchildren and great grandchildren and great-great grandchildren into slavery. In the same way, the effect of being obedient to God may last until the thousandth generation. By one act of love, you could have blessed a thousandth generation in your family. Which is better? Let me show you.

> *"You shall not make for yourself an idol in the form of anything in heaven above or on the earth beneath or in the waters below. You shall not bow down to them or worship them; for I, the LORD your God, am a jealous God, punishing the children for the sin of the fathers to the third and fourth generation of those who hate Me, but showing love to a thousand generation of those who love Me and keep my commandments" (Exodus 20:4-6, NIV).*

David McCullough in his book 'Mornings On Horseback' tells this story about young Teddy Roosevelt: Mittie (his mother) had found he was so afraid of the Madison Square Church that he refused to set foot inside if alone. He was terrified, she discovered, of something called the 'zeal.' It was crouched in the dark corners of the Church ready to jump at him, he said. When asked what 'zeal' might be, he said he was not sure, but thought it was probably a large animal like an alligator or a dragon. He had heard the minister read about it from the Bible. Using a concordance, Mittie read him those passages containing the word ZEAL until suddenly, very excited, he told her to stop. The line was from the Book of John, 2:17: "And his disciples remembered that it was written, 'The ZEAL of thine house hath eaten me up'! People are still justifiably afraid to come near the 'zeal' of the Lord, for they are perfectly aware it could "eat them up" if they are not one of His. Our Lord is good, but He isn't safe[3].

You need not fear the zeal of the house of the Lord. Many people fear things or creatures of God rather than God. The only One you need to fear is God. The reverent fear of the Lord will prevent you from wanting to do what you know will offend Him. If you love someone, you will do all that is in your power not to offend them. So we fear God out of reverence for Him, not because He holds a long white cane waiting for us to go wrong so He can punish us.

One time many years ago, the king of Hungary found himself depressed and unhappy. He sent for his brother, a good-natured but rather an indifferent prince. The king said to him, "I am a great sinner; I fear to meet God." However, the prince only laughed at him. This did not help the king's disposition. Though he was a believer, the king had gotten a glimpse of his guilt for the way he'd been living lately, and he sincerely wanted help. In those days, it was customary that if the executioner sounded a trumpet on a man's door at any hour, it was a signal that he was to be led to his execution. The king sent the executioner in the dead of the night to sound the fateful blast at his brother's door. The prince realised with horror what was happening. Quickly dressing, he stepped to the door and was seized by the executioner, and dragged pale and trembling into the king's presence. In an agony of terror, he fell on his knees before his brother and begged to know how he had offended him. "My brother," answered the king, "if the sight of a human executioner is so terrible to you, shall not I, having grievously offended God, fear to be brought before the judgment seat of Christ?"[4]

The fear of God will prevent you from selling out to the devil. What you will become has been predetermined but whether or not you will ever become it depends on you. Joseph's future was revealed to him while he was a teenager. It then took thirteen long years and a long winded route to get to the fulfilment of that destiny.

Had Joseph not feared God, the story could have been different, and the outcome could have been devastating for Joseph, his family and the entire people today referred to as the Hebrew nation. In the face of trials and tribulations, Joseph stood his ground and would not throw away the good upbringing and love legacy of his dad.

Joseph suffered for just over two years as a result of his refusal to enjoy a temporary pleasure with Potiphar's obsessed wife and compromise and sell his future because he feared God. He undoubtedly could have continued to enjoy free sex for some time which would have to come to an end one way or another, sooner than later. He would then have lost on every count and never become the leader that God intended him to become. You can read of this amazing true story in the book of Genesis from chapter 39 to 41. Let's read a bit of the story.

"Thus he left all that he had in Joseph's hand, and he did not know what he had except for the bread which he ate. Now Joseph was handsome in form and appearance. And it came to pass after these things that his master's wife cast longing eyes on Joseph, and she said, 'Lie with me.' But he refused and said to his master's wife, 'Look, my master does not know what is with me in the house, and he has committed all that he has to my hand. There is no one greater in this house than I, nor has he kept back anything from me but you, because you are his wife. How then can I do this great wickedness, and sin against God?'" (Genesis 39:6-9).

That was all. Altogether, Joseph suffered for 13 years. However, he gave life and sustenance to millions of Egyptians and hundreds of thousands of Israelites until their final exit out of Egypt 430 years later. What a gain and what a trade!

Please let me end this chapter with these two scriptures,

"Don't be impressed with your own wisdom. Instead, fear the LORD and turn away from evil" (Proverbs 3:7, NLT).

"One who is wise is cautious and turns away from evil, but a fool is reckless and careless" (Proverbs 14:16, ESV).

If only we know to what extent the effect of one act of disobedience will go, we will fear God. If only Adam, Abraham or David knew.

Key Points to Remember

- Serve God, now! Everything, you do, have consequences. If you serve Satan and become a slave to sin, it will lead to death. If you serve God and are His slave unto obedience, it leads to righteousness. If you do not get the results now, it will come later. If you do not pay for it, you may be paid for it.

- Do things so generations after you can praise your God. By one act of disobedience, you could have sold your children, grandchildren and great grandchildren and great-great grandchildren into slavery.
- Do you fear God? The fear of the Lord will prevent you from wanting to do what you know will offend Him. If you love someone, you will do all that is in your power not to offend them.

[1]Moody's Anecdotes, pp. 48-49.
[2]Harold Kellock, Houdini.
[3]David McCullough, Mornings on Horseback.
[4]Walk Through Rewards.

Chapter Two

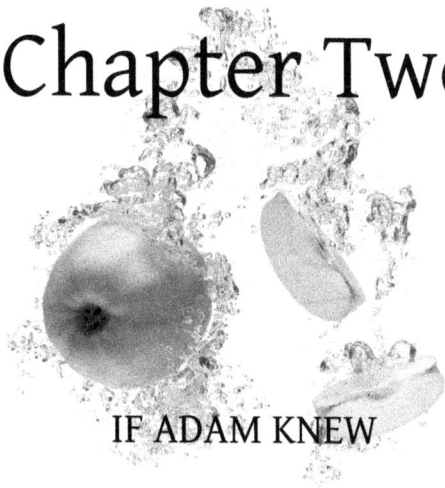

IF ADAM KNEW

Chapter Two

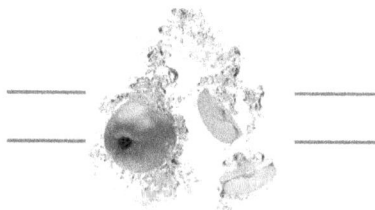

IF ADAM KNEW

The Dialogue

If Adam only knew that his disobedience would affect the whole world and how grievous the consequences would be, he probably would not have disobeyed God.

God asked Adam,

"... Where are you?"(Genesis 3:9).

That was not a quest for knowledge or education. God is omniscient; knowing all things. That also was not a question of physical location. God was only asking the man to make him think of his spiritual position. Adam was spiritually lost.

God had placed man in the highest of esteems, next only to Himself. In other words, man is subordinate only to God. This means we have been positioned higher than other heavenly beings, including angels.

"What is man that You take thought of him and the son of man that you care for him? Yet You have made him a little lower than God, and You crown him with glory and majesty!" (Psalms 8:4-5, NASB).

I have used the NASB because it came closest to the original Hebrew word translated 'angels' in the KJV. The actual word is 'Elohiym' used 2604 times in the entire Bible as; God (2346x), god (244x), judge (5x),   GOD (1x),   goddess (2x),   great (2x), mighty (2x), angels (1x) and exceeding (1x). The word is translated 'angels' only in the KJV of this passage. The error came from the Septuagint that replaced 'God' with 'angels'. Although, the translators got it wrong, this is how the KJV puts it.

"What is man, that thou art mindful of him, and the son of man, that thou visitest him? For thou hast made him a little lower than the angels, and hast crowned him with glory and honour" (Psalms 8:4-5, KJV).

God came to visit Adam "in the cool of the day" only to discover he was not in the spiritual position he was expected to be. Adam had left his privileged position of leadership, authority and dominion. He had allowed his worldly desire for power and equality (with God) to displace him from his position of rulership. His communion with God had been broken, and a spiritual gulf was created. Fear, loss of glory 'covering' and secrecy became part of human nature. The glory and majesty of God that covered Adam was uncovered, so he became naked, and because his innocence was stripped, he discovered his nakedness. Although Adam had been naked before the fall, he was not ashamed; he was innocent.

"And they were both naked, the man and his wife, and were not ashamed" (Genesis 2:25).

After the fall of the garden, men began to hide their true identity and nature from God and one another.

"He answered, 'I heard you in the garden, and I was afraid because I was naked; so I hid.'" (Genesis 3:10, NIV).

Over 6,000 years (150 generations) later, we are still suffering the consequences. Most of these consequences are listed below derived from the curses in Genesis 3:17-19 and a few other passages in the Bible.

Consequences of Adam's fall

- It grieves the heart of God (Genesis 6:5-7).
- It brings guilt, anxiety and insecurity (Genesis 3:8; Psalms 51:3-4).
- It results in separation from God (Genesis 3:8; Psalms 51:3-4).
- It brings judgement and everlasting punishment (Matthew 25:46).
- It enslaves (Romans 6:17).
- It causes spiritual blindness (2 Corinthians 4:4).
- It causes spiritual death (Ephesians 2:1).
- It produces a lack of hope (Ephesians 2:12).
- It corrupts (Titus 1:5).
- It condemns (James 5:12).
- It brings shame and fear (Genesis 3:10).
- It causes pain (Genesis 3:16).
- It brings servitude (Genesis 3:16).
- It causes sorrow (Genesis 3:17).
- It brings curses (Genesis 3:17-18).
- It brings sweat and toil (Genesis 3:19).
- It causes physical death (Genesis 3:19).
- It produces suffering (Romans 8:22).
- It causes sickness (Romans 8:18; Micah 6:13).

This is Too Much

I feel like jumping out of the pages of this book and screaming, "It is too much!" The consequences are too many for a little indulgence. It would be better to weigh the pleasure potentially derivable from disobedience against the immeasurable pain that must be endured by many. There are tens of thousands of diseases caused by the fall. For example, scientists currently estimate that over 10,000 of human diseases are known to be monogenic. Monogenic diseases result from modifications in a single gene occurring in all cells of the body. Though relatively rare, they affect millions of people worldwide[1]. This is not to mention 10,000s of other diseases known to man.

Many people are still in disobedience to the word of God and Christians are taking the lead. We disobey God in too many ways to count. We abuse His grace in the belief that 'morning by morning, His mercies' we would see continually. The Lord is asking us to avoid sin and disobedience rather than seek mercy all the time.

Sin is Attractive

I read about a family that visited the Niagara Falls several years ago. The season was spring, and the family noticed ice was flowing down the river. There they saw large blocks of ice rushing toward the falls and also discovered that carcasses of dead fish were embedded in the ice. Scores of Seagulls came riding down the river to feed on the dead fishes. Close to the time the ice would approach the edge of the fall, the Seagulls would stretch out their wings to fly and escape from falling.

There was, however one seagull that seemed to delay and the family wondered when it would leave. It was engrossed in the carcass of a fish, and when it finally came to the brink of the falls, out went its powerful wings. The bird flapped and flapped and even lifted the ice out of the water, and it was assumed it would soon escape. However, it had delayed too long so that its claws had frozen into the ice. The weight of the ice was too great, and the Seagull plunged into the abyss.

Sin is attractive, but it can also ensnare. It is easier to avoid its lure than to quit its grip. There is nothing the enemy will offer without compromise. It is usually harder to give up material possessions of this world or the pleasures of life once it has been tasted. Sins will take us to our destruction if we become too attached to them[2].

Let me Repeat

Had Adam known what we now know, he probably would have given more thought to his action. We know that what we do or omit to do knowing we are supposed to do might end up affecting four generations after us. Such knowledge was not available to Adam. The summary is this: The entire universe is suffering the consequences of Adam's wrong choices.

"For we know that the whole creation groans and labours with birth pangs together until now" (Romans 8:22).

The question that must now be answered is this: What would it take to reverse this catastrophe? The answer is found in Romans 8:19. We need to come out of hiding. We need to show up, step up and stand up. We manifest His power when we stop hiding and begin to establish God's kingdom here on earth.

"For the earnest expectation of the creature waiteth for the manifestation of the sons of God" (Romans 8:19, KJV).

Key Point to Remember

- Everyone will leave an inheritance for his or her children's children. The question is; what do you want your children to inherit. Is it the good or the bad? Make your mind up to stay away from what might yield a bad return for future generations.

[1]http://www.who.int/genomics/public/geneticdiseases/en/index2.html

[2]Adaptation of Dr. George Sweetings Special Sermons for Special Days.

Chapter Three

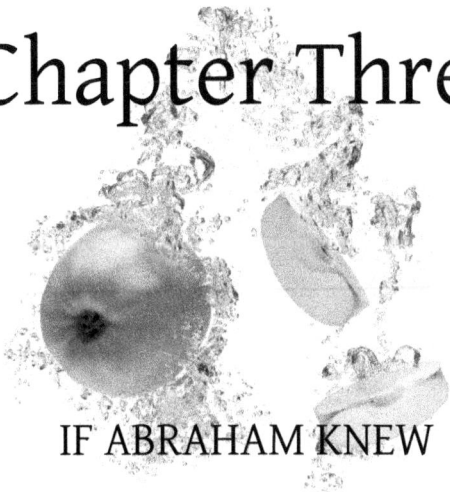

IF ABRAHAM KNEW

Chapter Three

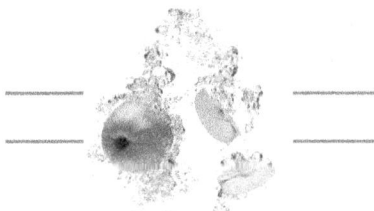

IF ABRAHAM KNEW

The Dialogue

While the sin of disobedience committed by Adam affected and still affects the whole world, another man's sin affected an entire nation. A disobedience may not affect the while world but it may affect a family. If Abraham only knew that his affair with Hagar would cause, to this day, an unending enmity between her seed and that of Sarah, he probably would not have had it. Let us look at some of the consequences of Abraham's compromise.

First of all, Abram suffered thirteen years of separation and silence from God. According to the

Bible, between 86 and 99 years of his life, heaven was silent.

> *"And Abram was eighty-six years old when Hagar bore him Ishmael. When Abram was ninety-nine years old, the LORD appeared to him and said, 'I AM God Almighty; walk before Me and be blameless'" (Genesis 16:16-17:1, NIV).*

Each time Abram would kneel to pray, he would encounter a dead silence. Heaven was a brass. God refused to speak to Abram haven demonstrated his inability to handle his family by allowing the society to influence him to the extent that he sinned against God.

Perhaps heaven is closed over your life because you have not kept to the previous instruction and agreement you had with God.

Secondly, Sarai was tormented and despised by her maid. What rights had a slave girl to treat her mistress in such a way, someone who gave her an undeserved privilege? Would it have been better for Sarai to remain childless than to be despised and humiliated by someone she called a servant?

Thinking about it, Sarai was only observing what was culturally acceptable. She was not looking for a mistress or someone with whom to share her marital home. No sensible woman would do that. It is amazing how what initially appeared innocent suddenly turned chaotic. It must have been difficult for Sarai to imagine her husband sharing his time with another woman, let alone her maid.

Hagar abused her privileges. She was excused from many slave duties so she could be physically, emotionally and sexually ready for Abram during the night hours. She was beginning to enjoy freedom and was gradually becoming emotionally attached to Abram. She started to dream of the possibility of permanently living in the palace as the only and rightful mother of the promised child. She thought for a moment of the possibility of Sarai remaining permanently childless. Of course, she could not show her feelings or share them with anyone. She could not even offend Madam Sarai. If she did, she could be quickly replaced by a more eligible alternative. She had to keep quiet 'until such a time.'

Then her moment came, the pregnancy test arrived positive. She had the scarce commodity. She may not be a valued slave, but she suddenly became an invaluable mother-to-be. She was able to give Abram what Sarai her mistress could not. For a moment, she thought, 'I am better than Sarai.' So she began to threaten abortion if Sarai did not cooperate or behave herself. Her privileged position got to her head, and Sarai was despised.

Sarai now wished she had been a little more patient. What is she now to do? She blamed everything on her husband for encouraging his desire and desperation for a son to affect him without giving thought to the consequence his action would have on her. She expected him to step in and protect her from being despised by her slave. When he did not, she became angry with him and picked a fight. Abram would not have that also. So he gave Sarai the responsibility to mete out any punishment to her maid deemed appropriate to her. The situation became so bad they could not be bothered about having a son anymore. Not with that kind of attitude from a slave anyway.

What Was Their Wrong?

Why should they suffer? What was their wrong? Such are the questions billions of people are asking without any hope of receiving any relevant answers. On our streets and in the pews are many people suffering for the sins of few, particularly those close to them. Majority do not know they are paying for something they did not purchase. They do not know why they have been singled out, or what could be done to get them out. What a tragedy?

What was her wrong? Hagar was a slave girl minding her business when she received summon. She would begin to wonder what wrong she had committed. Why was her mistress suddenly taking interest in her, amongst comparable options? Was any one of the slaves expecting such privilege, knowing the culture? When the time comes, who would be the favoured one? Did any of the slave girls do anything to get noticed knowing the likelihood of this happening – work harder maybe or dress more neatly? What was the reason Hagar was chosen? No one knows.

Hagar could not say 'No' even if she were not interested in the proposal. This too was a possibility. Knowing that Sarai was only interested in herself, Hagar could have been uninterested in the idea of using her as the mother of Sarah's adopted child. She could have felt violated, yet she could not refuse the offer. Otherwise, she could have been killed, sold or thrown out of the palace. Who knows what could have happened to a disobedient slave? So Hagar put her life in the hands of her master and mistress knowing she could never replace Sarai in Abram's heart or become the first wife though she were the first mother. She knew when push comes to shove; she would be the one to leave. As thought, it did, but she still had to comply.

Hagar reluctantly offered her body but not her soul. She would bear a child for Sarai but not without some form of reward. From now on, she would not wash plates or do the bedrooms. She would not do the laundry or mop the floor. She is now a wife. She would no longer submit to her mistress. So Sarai felt despised when Hagar refused to do the slave chores. Hagar was tormented and had misery as a result. However, she was not driven from home. When she could no longer endure the hardship, Hagar fled for her life; from misery and affliction.

> *"...Then Sarai mistreated Hagar; so she fled away. The Angel of the LORD said to her, "Return to your mistress, and submit yourself under her hand." The angel of the LORD also said to her: 'You are now with child and you will have a son. You shall call his name Ishmael, for the LORD has heard of your misery'"* (Genesis 16:6, 9, 11, NIV).

Hagar then received a warning by the angel she encountered. So she went back home to her mistress in the hope God was going to sort things out. However, things got worse. Later we read of a 26-year old man enjoying the pleasure in tormenting his 12-year old sibling. Imagine a young boy being tormented by a brother more than twice his age for sins he did not commit. This was no token sibling rivalry; it was tormenting of the highest degree. It was so bad God's attention was required, and excommunication was the given verdict. On this occasion, Hagar was thrown out with her son.

> *"The child grew and was weaned, and on the day Isaac was weaned Abraham held a great feast. But Sarah saw that the son whom Hagar the Egyptian had borne to Abraham was mocking, and she said to Abraham, 'Get rid of that slave woman and her son, for that slave woman's son will never share in the inheritance with my son Isaac.' The matter displeased Abraham greatly because it concerned his son. But God said to him, 'Do not be so distressed about the boy and your maidservant. Listen to whatever Sarah tells you, because it is through Isaac that your offspring will be reckoned. I will make the son of the maidservant into a nation also, because he is your offspring. Early the next morning Abraham took some food and a skin of water and gave them to Hagar. He set them on her shoulders and then sent her off with the boy. She went on her way and wandered in the desert of Beersheba" (Genesis 21:8-14, NIV).*

The two halves of 26 years must have been tormenting for Hagar. During the first 13 years,

Hagar lived the life of a wife valued only for her body and the next 13 years, fighting for the rights of her innocent son. She got battered from all angles by her mistress.

What about Ishmael? Though he scoffed at his brother, he was himself a victim of the situation. He did not choose to be born to a family struggling to keep their heads up in a society that says your family is not complete unless you buy, beg or steal a child, adopt or give birth to one. They lived in a society that valued women not for their worth, but for their ability to conceive and birth choice children at their desired time; an insane society similar to what exists even in the 21st Century.

Come to think of it, who would blame Ishmael? He grew up in his first 13 years thinking and living the life of a promised seed in the palace of Abraham. He had the entire wealth of his father to himself. His father cherished and nourished him as his only son to the point that he was even displeased with the thought of him leaving home. He might not have been a child of choice, but he was a child to choose nonetheless. Perhaps he even knew he was not the promised child yet he grew up as the only one. Beside him there was no other. Even 13 years after his birth, Sarai still could not conceive, and so the hope of the choice child was gone.

The second positive pregnancy test in the life of Abraham occurred before his death. Nine months later, Isaac was miraculously born when Ishmael was in his second teenage year – 14 years old. All hopes disappeared. Hopes of being the heir apparent; the right to the palace and the right of the firstborn were in a moment lost. For the next 12 years, things were never going to be the same. As Isaac started growing up, Ishmael began to realise his special privileges would soon begin to diminish and eventually taken away. What could he have done? So he began to scoff.

We have seen that Abraham's sin was not only punished on Abraham but his entire family. Sarah was despised, and so were Isaac, Ishmael and Hagar.

The Whole World Groans

"The Scriptures say that Abraham had two sons, one from his slave-wife and one from his freeborn wife. The son of the slave-wife was born in a human attempt to bring about the fulfilment of God's promise. But the son of the freeborn wife was born as God's own fulfilment of His promise. Now these two women serve as an illustration of God's two covenants. Hagar, the slave-wife, represents Mount Sinai where

people first became enslaved to the law. And now Jerusalem is just like Mount Sinai in Arabia, because she and her children live in slavery. But Sarah, the free woman, represents the heavenly Jerusalem. And she is our mother. That is what Isaiah meant when he prophesied, 'Rejoice, O childless woman! Break forth into loud and joyful song, even though you never gave birth to a child. For the woman who could bear no children now has more than all the other women.' And you dear brothers and sisters are children of the promise, just like Isaac. And we who are born of the Holy Spirit are persecuted by those who want us to keep by Ishmael, the son of the slave-wife. But what do the Scriptures say about that? 'Get rid of the slave and her son, for the son of the slave woman will not share the family inheritance with the free woman's son.' So, dear brothers and sisters, we are not children of the slave woman, obligated to the law. We are children of the free woman, acceptable to God because of our faith" (Galatians 4:21-31, NLT).

The summary of the scripture above is this. The problem in the Middle East today is because of the human attempt to bring about the fulfilment of

God's promise. Paul hit the nail on the head. It cannot be simpler than that.

We sometimes think of how to help God. Since He lives in heaven, we think He probably does not understand our pains and frustrations. God does not need our help to fulfil His promises. He is sovereign, omnipotent and all-sufficient. We end up complicating our situations and mess up when we try to help God. After Abraham had attempted to help God, he received a stark warning.

"...I AM God Almighty; walk before Me and be blameless" (Genesis 17:1, NIV).

Part of the cure for sin is obedience. However, obedience alone is not enough. The permanent cure for sin includes walking before God. We sometimes walk with God. After that, we follow God. We need to progress to walking before God. When we do, He can keep us under His watchful eyes. Not that He cannot see us wherever we may be, but we need to place ourselves under His scrutiny. We do this by finding out what displeases Him through reading His word and keeping it at the centre of our hearts.

"How can a young person stay pure? By obeying Your word and following its rules. I have tried my best to find you - don't let me wander from

your commands. I have hidden Your word in my heart, that I might not sin against You" (Psalms 119:9-11, NLT).

We stay away from sin by the observance of the word of God but prevent going into sin by finding out what God says about it in the first place. Abraham did not stay away from sin, and as a result, the lives of many innocent souls were affected.

You may be suffering the consequence of things you knew nothing about; may be of parents or guardians; may be from governing authorities of your country; there is hope for you. You can be set free. You do not have to live with it for the rest of your life. Ask God to forgive your ancestors where the offences are known and ask Him to set you free. Where restitution is appropriate and affordable, you may need to do so. This must be done with the utmost sensitivity. If you feel overwhelmed by the burden, share it with your spiritual leader and God will grant unto you liberty and freedom.

Key Points to Remember

- Don't be too impatient to the point you displease God in order to please the society. It is better to please God than look good to the world. Don't be a people pleaser. It is better to die with honour before God than to live with honour before men.

- As a worker, employee, staff or servant, do not abuse your privileges. Your position gives you no rights to dishonour your superiors.

- Let not your position of leadership become a tool to torment younger siblings as Ishmael did to Isaac. They are there to be looked after, not laughed at.

- Ask God to give you the wisdom to deal with the love or hate situation with your children without being partial or taking sides.

- If you are a victim of bad parenting or government, you can be set free. Ask God to forgive your ancestors where the offences are known and ask Him to set you free. If you feel overwhelmed by the burden, share it with your spiritual leader and God will grant unto you liberty and freedom.

- Don't try to help God like Abram and Sarai. God does not need our assistance to bring about the manifestation of His promises in our lives.

Chapter Four

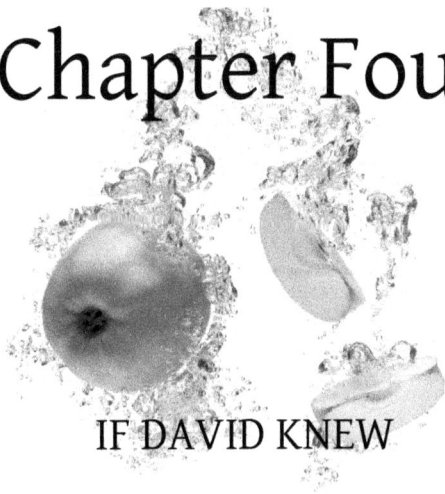

IF DAVID KNEW

Chapter Four

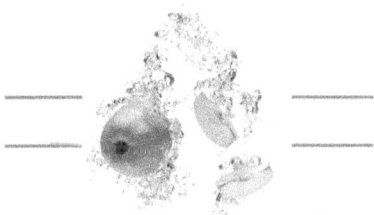

IF DAVID KNEW

Adam's disobedience affected the whole world, and Abraham's impatience affected the Hebrew race primarily, but for David, his family would feel the consequences of his sin.

In the Book of Esther, one night with the king brought deliverance to the Jewish nation. However, in the Book of 2 Samuel, one night with the king brought a curse on a family. David's one night with Bathsheba had dire consequences. It costs his family dearly. You can read the entire story in 2 Samuel 11 and 12.

First it resulted in the death of an innocent warrior, Uriah, Bathsheba's husband.

"In the morning it happened that David wrote a letter to Joab and sent it by the hand of Uriah. And he wrote in the letter, saying, 'Set Uriah in the forefront of the hottest battle, and retreat from him, that he may be struck down and die.' So it was, while Joab besieged the city, that he assigned Uriah to a place where he knew there were valiant men. Then the men of the city came out and fought with Joab. And some of the people of the servants of David fell; and Uriah the Hittite died also" (2 Samuel 11:14-17).

Secondly, it resulted in the death of an innocent baby David fathered out of adultery.

"When David saw that his servants were whispering, David perceived that the child was dead. Therefore, David said to his servants, 'Is the child dead?' And they said, 'He is dead'" (2 Samuel 12:19).

Thirdly, there was a curse placed on the family. From then on, the family was going to be perpetually attacked, and there were going to be constant battles within and without. They were to be fighting each other within and warring and warding away enemies without.

"'Now therefore, the sword shall never depart from your house, because you have despised Me,

and have taken the wife of Uriah the Hittite to be your wife.' Thus says the LORD: 'Behold, I will raise up adversity against you from your own house; and I will take your wives before your eyes and give them to your neighbour, and he shall lie with your wives in the sight of this sun. 'For you did it secretly, but I will do this thing before all Israel, before the sun'" (2 Samuel 12:10-12).

There were also going to be humiliation and disgrace by David's son. The dynasty was going to be dishonoured, and royalty besmirched. As was foretold by the prophet Nathan, Absalom publicly slept with David's concubines.

"And Ahithophel said to Absalom, 'Go in to your father's concubines, whom he has left to keep the house; and all Israel will hear that you are abhorred by your father. Then the hands of all who are with you will be strong.' So they pitched a tent for Absalom on the top of the house, and Absalom went in to his father's concubines in the sight of all Israel. Now the advice of Ahithophel, which he gave in those days, was as if one had inquired at the oracle of God. So was all the advice of Ahithophel both with David and with Absalom" (2 Samuel 16:21-23).

The penalty for any offence in many cases always outweighs the temporary pleasures that may have been derived from it. Also, the punishment usually outlives the offender and many innocent generations after may be infected or affected or both. We should allow the Spirit of God to illuminate our hearts and reveal to us the dangers of our ungodly and immoral actions irrespective of what the world around us believes.

So how can you prevent all these calamities and protect your future? I will discuss this in the next chapter.

Key Points to Remember

- Ask God to direct your path. David was at the wrong place at the wrong time. He was supposed to be at the battle ground but was instead on the rooftop of his palace.
- Run from temptations. Looking once is not a sin, looking a second time is.
- Do not use your position of authority to manipulate or force others to do what in the natural is against their will. It is an abuse of position.
- Think of your loved ones that may be affected by your actions before you do it.

Chapter Five

HIS TACTICS ARE
STIIL THE SAME

Chapter Five

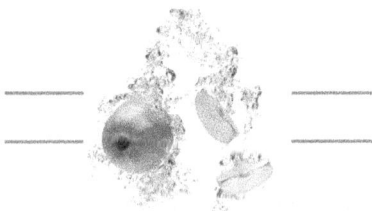

HIS TACTICS ARE STILL THE SAME

He Lurks in the Dark

Derek Curtis Bok, a lawyer, educator and the former president of Harvard University once said this: "If you think education is expensive, try ignorance." He was right. Ignorance can be more expensive than education. It is wrong to say that what you do not know cannot hurt you. It can. If you are unaware of your rights as a child of God, the devil will take advantage of you.

"Lest Satan should take advantage of us; for we are not ignorant of his devices" (2 Corinthians 2:11).

It is the devil's deliberate act to keep Christians ignorant. Ignorance is his greatest and most potent weapon. He would do all that is in his power to make and keep people ignorant. He keeps people in the dark and blinds the eyes of the seekers.

"Whose minds the god of this age has blinded, who do not believe, lest the light of the gospel of the glory of Christ, who is the image of God, should shine on them" (2 Corinthians 4:4).

The devil lurks and lives in the dark. He lies in wait, skulks, prowls, loiters, hangs about and creeps around in the dark recesses of our life. No wonder most evils are done in the dark. Do not be fooled when the devil appear as your helper and pretend to be the angel of light. He is still the prince of this dark world.

"And no wonder! For Satan himself transforms himself into an angel of light" (2 Corinthians 11:14).

He is Deceptive

The devil is a deceiver. His other classic vice is deception. That is why he is called the "father of lies." Lying or deception is his second nature. This guy is crafty.

"But I fear, lest somehow, as the serpent deceived Eve by his craftiness, so your minds may be corrupted from the simplicity that is in Christ" *(2 Corinthians 11:3).*

"For Adam was formed first, then Eve. And Adam was not deceived, but the woman being deceived, fell into transgression" (1 Timothy 2:13-14).

Paul said Adam was not deceived. No, he could not be deceived. Adam was not deceived because he could not be deceived. Deception can only happen where the "truth" is not known or not fully understood. It will take much effort for someone to be persuaded that the green apple he or she is holding is actually a red apple unless he or she does not understand colours very well. Where the devil senses the smallest degree of uncertainty, he would then plant doubt. He made Eve doubt God's instruction because he measured her depth of comprehension of the command not to eat of the fruit of the tree in the midst of the garden and perhaps found it was flawed.

*"Now the serpent was **MORE CUNNING** than any beast of the field which the LORD God had made. And he said to the woman, "Has God **INDEED** said, 'You shall not eat of every tree of the garden'?" (Genesis 3:1).*

It was a lot easier to deceive Eve. She either did not fully grasp what the command was or did not realise the gravity of the offence. The command not to eat of the fruit of the tree in the midst of the garden was not directly given to her. It must have been relayed to her by Adam.

So Satan went for Eve and deliberately avoided any confrontation with Adam. The devil knew Adam would have told him straight away what God's instruction was. When Adam ate the forbidden fruit, his action was not in any way of an omission. Rather, it was an act of disobedience.

Paradoxically, it may still be possible for someone to sin even with the knowledge of the truth. This happens when someone ignores the consequences of his or her action. This is not usually a result of deception, but it is based on the promise of a higher reward for the disobedience; in this case, the promised of attaining god-ship.

The devil still promises people all sorts today – fame, fortune and fantasies. You could be his next target.

He is a Master Planner

The devil is a strategist par excellence. He is a schemer and a thinker. He plans, plots and executes those plans to a fault. He does not like to hit and miss. Although he is an opportunist, he can wait for as long as it would take before launching an attack. Take a look at this;

> *"Lest Satan should take advantage of us; for we are not ignorant of his **devices**" (2 Corinthians 2:11).*

The word 'devices' is the Greek word 'noēma.' Other translations used the word thoughts, schemes and designs. The word occurs six times in the New Testament. Four times 'noēma' was translated as 'minds', once as 'devices' and once as 'thoughts.' For a better understanding of the word, I will list the other five scriptures.

> *"But their **minds** were blinded. For until this day the same veil remains unlifted in the reading of the Old Testament, because the veil is taken away in Christ" (2 Corinthians 3:14).*

> *"Whose **minds** the god of this age has blinded, who do not believe, lest the light of the gospel of the glory of Christ, who is the image of God, should shine on them" (2 Corinthians 4:4).*

> *"But I fear, lest somehow, as the serpent deceived Eve by his craftiness, so your **minds** may be corrupted from the simplicity that is in Christ" (2 Corinthians 11:3).*

"And the peace of God, which surpasses all understanding, will guard your hearts and <u>minds</u> through Christ Jesus" (Philippians 4:7).

"Casting down arguments and every high thing that exalts itself against the knowledge of God, bringing <u>every thought</u> into captivity to the obedience of Christ" (2 Corinthians 10:5).

Did you notice that all but one of the six scriptures spoke with respect to spiritual warfare, focusing on thoughts and minds? Satan's schemes are his thoughts and minds. This is why I said he is a strategist par excellence. To defeat the devil, we would then need to think on a higher dimension. We cannot think like him; we have to think like Christ. The battlefield is our minds. That is where we can be defeated or exalted.

We would not allow the devil to infiltrate us with junk. We would not buy his suggestions and lies. We would focus our minds on things that are above which are eternal and not on things beneath which are temporal. We would let our minds follow after God and things that are godly. We cannot and will not be defeated by the devil. We are smarter than he is. We are of God. We would cast down arguments and every high thing that exalts itself against the knowledge of God. We operate on a higher dimension. We would beat the strategist par excellence at his own game. We are not fighting like ones beating the air. We would prevail, not in our strength, but through Him who strengthen us. Where we have failed, we would look back and launch higher. We are overcomers and more than conquerors. Amen.

Other Scriptures about Ignorance

"For I do not desire, brethren, that you should be ignorant of this mystery, lest you should be wise in your own opinion, that blindness in part has happened to Israel until the fullness of the Gentiles has come in" (Romans 11:25).

"Now concerning spiritual gifts, brethren, I do not want you to be ignorant:" (1 Corinthians 12:1).

"Having their understanding darkened, being alienated from the life of God, because of the ignorance that is in them, because of the blindness of their heart;" (Ephesians 4:18).

Key Points to Remember

- Acquire the facts. It is wrong to say that what you do not know cannot hurt you. It can.

- Confirm the facts. Where the devil senses the smallest degree of uncertainty, he would then plant doubt.

- Process the facts. The battlefield is our minds. To defeat the devil, you have to think on a higher dimension.

- Delete the wrong facts. We would not allow the devil to infiltrate us with junk. We would cast down arguments and every high thing that exalts itself against the knowledge of God.

- Store the right facts. We would let our minds follow after God and things that are godly.

Chapter Six

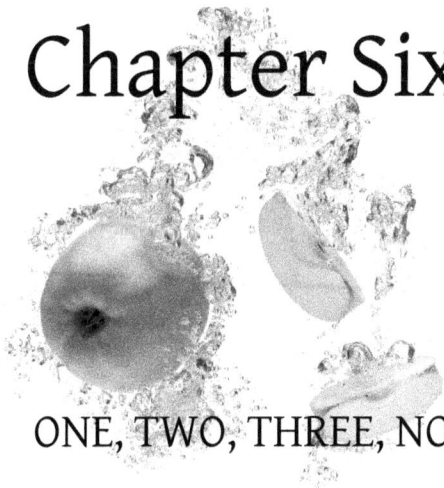

ONE, TWO, THREE, NO

Chapter Six

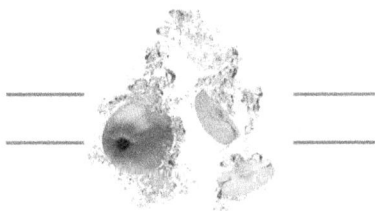

ONE, TWO, THREE, NO

One: The Lust of the Eyes. Two: The Lust of the Flesh. Three: The Pride of Life. After that is, NO.

Satan has an agenda. His aim is to push his agenda until his targets succumb. In the last chapter, we saw who Satan is but we would now see how he operates in the life of the believer. The scripture below sums up the devil's old tricks. If you can say 'NO' to him in these three areas, you will never again be conquered. That is why I titled this chapter, "One, Two, Three, 'NO.'" Here it goes;

"Do not love the world or the things in the world. If anyone loves the world, the love of the Father is not in him. For all that is in the world – the lust of the flesh, the lust of the eyes, and the pride of life – is not of the Father but is of the world. And the world is passing away, and the lust of it; but he who does the will of God abides forever" (1 John 2:15-17).

The Lust of the Flesh

The lust of the flesh is simply the cravings or desires of the body. Our bodies have need for food, drink, touch, intimacy, healing, and more. Although these are general necessities of life, they can also become problems in that we can fall prey of its lusting. Lusting is craving for the forbidden rather than the allowed. Love is a wholesome desire, whereas lust is a perverted one. Lust seeks after fornication or adultery, gluttony, alternate medicine, etc. Basically, body needs and desires met through the wrong channels constitute lust. When we succumb to the demands of the flesh, we make the devil the winner.

Thomas Costain's history, *The Three Edwards*, described the life of Raynald III, a fourteenth-century duke in what is now Belgium. Grossly overweight, Raynald was commonly called by his Latin nickname, Crassus, which means "fat."

After a violent quarrel, Raynald's younger brother Edward led a successful revolt against him. Edward captured Raynald but did not kill him. Instead, he built a room around Raynald in the Nieuwkerk castle and promised him he could regain his title and property as soon as he was able to leave the room.

This would not have been difficult for most people since the room had several windows and a door of near-normal size, and none was locked or barred. The problem was Raynald's size. To regain his freedom, he needed to lose weight. However, Edward knew his older brother, and each day he sent a variety of delicious foods. Instead of dieting his way out of prison, Raynald grew fatter.

When Duke Edward was accused of cruelty, he had a ready answer: "My brother is not a prisoner. He may leave when he so wills." Raynald stayed in that room for ten years and wasn't released until after Edward died in battle. By then his health was so ruined he died within a year. Raynald was a prisoner of his own appetite[1].

A genuinely redeemed child of God does not yield to the dictates of the flesh. This is not saying that he or she might not be tempted, just that he masters his desires and would not allow the body to dominate or rule. We have the power to refuse the devil's suggestions to lust. To claim to be in the spirit and yielding to the demands of the flesh is a contradiction in terms.

> *"I say then: Walk in the Spirit, and you shall not fulfill the lust of the flesh. For the flesh lusts against the Spirit, and the Spirit against the flesh; and these are contrary to one another, so that you do not do the things that you wish. But if you are led by the Spirit, you are not under the law" (Galatians 5:16-18).*

The Lust of the Eyes

The devil uses a similar method when it comes to the eyes. We appreciate the wonders of God's creation and behold with awe the beauty of His love through the things we observe with our eyes. The tool God gave can be used for bad cause when we permit the devil its control. The God-given ability for vision is a good thing that can be used in love and to further a good cause. The same in Satan's hand can become a lust tool. He is well aware of damages he can exert using our eyes against us. Just take a look at the media; the internet, the television, the papers, the lights at the casinos and the ornate presentations in the windows. Why do you think nudity is being normalised? Sex sells for a reason. We are being drawn to many lustful things in the things we see.

The Pride of Life

Let's face it; we all take pride in our achievements and possessions. We show off with the certificates on our walls both at home and in our offices. Some list the titles after their names and others, before their names. Our business cards, our cell phones and our cars are today's status symbols. We pride ourselves in the knowledge we possess and our educational achievements. Coated in immodesty, vanity, self-importance, smugness, conceit, egotism, vanity, arrogance and feelings of superiority, pride destroys. It is the temptation to want to be our own boss, the need to be in charge of our lives. It is the temptation to want to be valued and be self-sufficient leading to pride and boasting.

These are the things – the lust of the flesh, the lust of the eyes and the pride of life – that comes between us and God. They may be three, but just one is strong enough to derail us and put us at odds with God, and the devil does not have to use the three before we become enemies of our creator. However, in most cases, the enemy of your soul will combine the three assaults to secure your capture. He did it to Eve, Potiphar's wife, Achan, David, but could not succeed with our Lord Jesus.

Key Points to Remember

- If you can say 'NO' to the devil, you will never again be conquered.
- Do not yield to the dictates of the flesh. Lusting is craving for the forbidden rather than the allowed.
- Master your desires and do not allow the body to dominate or rule.
- *Walk in the Spirit, and you shall not fulfill the lust of the flesh.*
- Watch what you watch. Not everything you see is good. You can be drawn to many lustful things in the things you see.
- Do not be prideful. Pride is the need to be in charge of our lives. It is the temptation to want to be valued and be self-sufficient.

[1]Dave Wilkenson

Chapter Seven

WE'VE SEEN THIS BEFORE

Chapter Seven

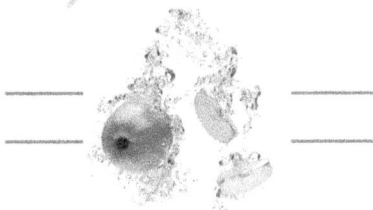

WE'VE SEEN THIS BEFORE

Satan is predictable. He doesn't have new tricks. He is not innovative, and neither is he creative. All he does is to remodel and repackage himself. From the day time began and until now, he is still using the same old tricks. Shouldn't we have known; shouldn't we have learnt?

The scripture below sums up the devil's old tricks;

> *"Do not love the world or the things in the world. If anyone loves the world, the love of the Father is not in him. For all that is in the world* **– the lust of the flesh, the lust of the eyes, and**

the pride of life – *is not of the Father but is of the world. And the world is passing away, and the lust of it; but he who does the will of God abides forever"* (1 John 2:15-17).

Whatever we strongly desire can become the route to our downfall. Desires are not in themselves wrong but Satan can capitalise on the strong desires, and it then becomes desperation. Desperation may then lead to compromise. This then becomes a weakness of the flesh and turns to become a stronghold. However, if you are aware of the devil's tricks, you can gain an understanding of the ways to prevent the desire to be taken advantage of.

As I hope to show from Bible passages, the New Covenant believers have an advantage the Old Covenant believers did not. We can see the devil at work. Come with me, and I will show you what the Bible say about this adversary.

The following people were tempted the same way, and I think their temptations teach us a great deal about the schemes of the devil seen in the previous chapter. It follows a pattern; the lust of the eyes (the sight), the lust of the flesh (the desire), and the pride of life (the pursuit).

Eve's Temptation

Adam and Eve were given the rare privilege of feeding on the lush provided in the Garden of Eden. There was however a tree of which they were forbidden to eat of its fruit. That was the one right in the middle of the garden – the tree of the knowledge of good and evil. Remember, I said earlier that Eve did not receive the instruction directly from God; her husband told her of God's wish. This gave Satan the opportunity to strike. So he went to the woman. Read with me how she responded to the Devil's proposition.

> *"When the woman saw that the fruit of the tree was good for food and pleasing to the eye, and also **desirable** for gaining wisdom, she **took** some and ate it. She also gave some to her husband, who was with her, and he ate it"* *(Genesis 3:6 NIV).*

> *"The woman was convinced. She **saw** that the tree was beautiful and its fruit **looked** delicious, and she wanted the wisdom it would give her. So she took some of the fruit and ate it. Then she gave some to her husband, who was with her, and he ate it, too" (Genesis 3:6 NLT).*

Sight, desire and pursuit are going to be the pattern used by the devil, both in this instance and those that will follow until the end of time.

- Sight – "She **saw** that the tree was beautiful, and its fruit **looked** delicious," (NLT)
- Desire – "and also **desirable** for gaining wisdom," (NIV)
- Pursuit – "she **took** some and ate it." (NIV)

Lot's Temptation

Contrary to God's express instruction (Genesis Chapter 12), Abram took Lot his nephew with him on a journey to a strange land. Both their businesses grew and were too big for the location south of Bethel. So their herdsmen began to fight for resources to take care of their growing flock. This led to the squabble between Abram and his nephew. Being the older, Abram yielded his ground and offered Lot the opportunity to be the first to choose from the vast land that surrounded them. Let us follow from Lot's response.

*Lot **took a long look** at the fertile plains of the Jordan Valley in the direction of Zoar. The whole area was well watered everywhere, **like the garden of the LORD** or the beautiful land of Egypt. (This* *was before the LORD destroyed Sodom and Gomorrah.) Lot chose for himself the whole Jordan Valley to the east of them. He went there with his flocks and servants and parted company with his uncle Abram" (Genesis 13:10-11 NLT).*

*"Lot looked. He saw the whole plain of the Jordan spread out, well watered (this was before GOD destroyed Sodom and Gomorrah), like GOD's garden, like Egypt, and stretching all the way to Zoar. Lot **took** the whole plain of the Jordan. Lot set out to the east" (Genesis 13:10-11, MSG).*

Did you see the pattern again in this discourse; the sight, desire and pursuit?

- Sight – "Lot **took a long look** at the fertile plains ..." (NLT)
- Desire – "whole area was well watered everywhere, **like the garden** of the LORD or the beautiful land of Egypt." (NLT)
- Pursuit – "Lot **took** the whole plain of the Jordan." (MSG)

Mrs. Potiphar's Temptation

Joseph was sold into slavery by his brothers because they could not handle the discovery that he was going to become their future leader being the eleventh son of Jacob. Arriving Egypt, he found himself serving under Pharaoh's Captain-of-the Guard, named Potiphar. There was an exchange between Joseph and Mrs. Potiphar. This is where we pick the story up.

Contrary to many teachings regarding Joseph being tempted, it is nowhere recorded that he entertained any desire for Mrs. Potiphar in his brief spell at her residence. The story was about Potiphar's wife, not about Joseph. She was the one who had a crush on Joseph. The story is found in Genesis 39:6-12.

> "Thus he left all that he had in Joseph's hand, and he did not know what he had except for the bread which he ate. Now Joseph was handsome in form and appearance. And it came to pass after these things that his master's wife **cast longing eyes** on Joseph, and **she said**, "Lie with me." But he refused and said to his master's wife, "Look, my master does not know what is with me in the house, and he has committed all that he has to my hand. There is no one greater in this house than I, nor has he kept back anything from me but you, because you are his wife. How then can I do this great wickedness, and sin against God?" So it was, as she **spoke** to Joseph day by day, that he did not heed her, to lie with her or to be with her. But it happened

*about this time, when Joseph went into the house to do his work, and none of the men of the house was inside, that she **caught** him by his garment, saying, "Lie with me." But he left his garment in her hand, and fled and ran outside"* (Genesis 39:6-12).

Although Joseph was *'handsome in form and appearance,'* *'he refused'* Mrs. Potiphar's hit on him, gave a reason for his refusal, considered yielding as a *'great wickedness, and sin against God,'* and fled when harassed. This does not look like someone who was tempted. Though he was raised in a polygamous environment, he had the fear of God and had conquered 'youthful lust.'

Let us now look at the reasons I concluded that it was Mrs. Potiphar's that was tempted. It fitted perfectly into the same pattern we have seen so far.

- Sight – "... his master's (Potiphar's) wife **cast longing eyes** on Joseph,"
- Desire – "... and **she said**, 'Lie with me.'" And "... she **spoke** to Joseph day by day,"
- Pursuit – "... she **caught** him by his garment,"

Achan's Temptation

The setting is the lost battle of Ai. The Children of Israel conquered Jericho, but someone took what was set apart for the Lord. Achan was exposed as the perpetrator. Here is his explanation.

*"When I **saw** among the spoils a beautiful Babylonian garment, two hundred shekels of silver, and a wedge of gold weighing fifty shekels, I **coveted** them and **took** them. And there they are, hidden in the earth in the midst of my tent, with the silver under it" (Joshua 7:21).*

Achan's temptation was not going to be different from our pattern of sight, desire and pursuit. We have seen this before. Amazing isn't it?

- Sight – "When I **saw** among the spoils a beautiful Babylonian garment, two hundred shekels of silver, and a wedge of gold weighing fifty shekels,"
- Desire – "I **coveted** them ..."
- Pursuit – "... and **took** them."

David's Temptation

"In the spring, at the time when kings go off to war, David sent Joab out with the king's men and the whole Israelite army. They destroyed the Ammonites and besieged Rabbah. But David remained in Jerusalem" (2 Samuel 11:1, NIV).

That was the setting – a king refusing to go to war when he was supposed to. See what happened next.

> *"Late one afternoon, after his midday rest, David got out of bed and was walking on the roof of the palace. As he **looked** out over the city, he **noticed** a woman of unusual beauty taking a bath. He sent **someone to find out** who she was, and he was told, "She is Bathsheba, the daughter of Eliam and the wife of Uriah the Hittite. Then David **sent messengers to get her**; and when she came to the palace, he **slept with her**. She had just completed the purification rites after having her menstrual period. Then she returned home"* (2 Samuel 11:2-4, NLT).*

- Sight – "As he **looked** out over the city, he **noticed** a woman of unusual beauty taking a bath."
- Desire – "He **sent someone to find out** who she was, and he was told,"
- Pursuit - "Then David **sent messengers to get her**; and when she came to the palace, he **slept with her**."

What a fall? It's the same pattern, again.

Child of God, Satan has not got any new strategy except to disguise the same one he is used to all these years. Watch what you see, it may turn to a strong desire that may then cause you to fall. The lust of the eyes, the lust of the flesh and the pride of life are the only ways Satan can get you. James put it succinctly in James 1:13-15,

> "Let no one say when he is tempted, "I am tempted by God"; for God cannot be tempted by evil, nor does He Himself tempt anyone. But each one is tempted when he is drawn away by his own desires and enticed. Then, when desire has conceived, it gives birth to sin; and sin, when it is full-grown, brings forth death" (James 1:13-15).

What about Jesus?

The devil is no respecter of persons. He went for the big boss. Our Lord Jesus Christ was not exempt from attacks. You would however have thought Satan would use a different tactic when he came to Jesus, but you see, it is not in him to innovate. In order to destroy God's plan for man's redemption, what Satan tried and succeeded with Eve, Lot, Mrs. Potiphar, Achan, and David, were to be tried on Jesus.

Jesus' Temptation

"Then Jesus was led up by the Spirit into the wilderness to be tempted by the devil. And when He had fasted forty days and forty nights, afterward He was hungry" (Matthew 4:1-2).

This is the background to the whole story. After fasting forty days and forty nights, it was natural for Jesus to feel hungry. That was the desire Satan needed to see so he can take advantage of Jesus. Remember, it was through food that Adam lost. It just happened that the devil's defeat was to come through food. Fortunately, what the first Adam could not resist, the second Adam could not consent. Let's read on.

Jesus Repressed His hunger (desire)

Although Jesus was hungry, dining with the devil was not an option. Jesus had to repress His hunger. You do not have to eat just anything because you are hungry. So many people have dipped their hands into the same plate the devil is eating from and they are direly paying for it. Several of our failings may be avoided if only we can defer our want to another time.

"Now when the tempter came to Him, he said, "If You are the Son of God, command that these stones become bread." But He answered and said, "It is written, 'Man shall not live by bread alone, but by every word that proceeds from the mouth of God'" (Matthew 4:3-4).

Jesus Rebuffs the Pursuit

Knowing who you are is essential to not yielding to what others suggest you should be. A healthy self-image will help you to not want to prove your worth. When the devil suggested to Jesus to jump, there was no need to question what the reactions of the angels would have been. They would show up. However, Jesus would have lost the battle to the devil because He would from then on be subject to him.

"Then the devil took Him up into the holy city, set Him on the pinnacle of the temple, and said to Him, "If You are the Son of God, throw Yourself down. For it is written: 'He shall give His angels charge over you,' and, 'In their hands they shall bear you up, lest you dash your foot against a stone.'" Jesus said to him, "It is written again, 'You shall not tempt the LORD your God'" (Matthew 4:5-7).

Jesus Refused to look (Sight)

Seen so far, most temptations started with sighting a desirable object or person. In the encounter with Jesus, the Master declined when Satan showed Him all the kingdoms of the world.

"Again, the devil took Him up on an exceedingly high mountain, and showed Him all the kingdoms of the world and their glory. And he said to Him, "All these things I will give You if You will fall down and worship me." Then Jesus said to him, "Away with you, Satan! For it is written, 'You shall worship the LORD your God, and Him only you shall serve.'" Then the devil left Him, and behold, angels came and ministered to Him" (Matthew 4:8-11).

Key Points to Remember

- Study yourself so you know where Satan can tempt you. He is predictable. He doesn't have new tricks.
- Refuse to be desperate for anything. If you cannot have it, you do not need it.
- Satanic Temptation follows a pattern; the lust of the eyes (the sight), the lust of the flesh (the desire), and the pride of life (the pursuit).

- Be careful; sight, desire and pursuit are going to be the pattern used by the devil.
- You do not have to satisfy every desire. Several of our failings may be avoided if only we can defer our want to another time.
- Knowing who you are is essential to not yielding to what others suggest you should be. A healthy self-image will help you to not want to prove your worth.

Chapter Eight

HOW TO PROTECT YOUR SPIRIT

Chapter Eight

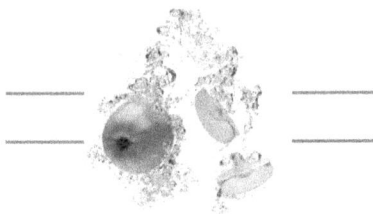

HOW TO PROTECT YOUR SPIRIT

Recognise and identify the areas of weaknesses

It is dangerous not to be aware of the areas you are weak. I am surprised when people say they do not know their areas of weaknesses. Do you know yours? Let's find out.

Have you ever committed fornication or adultery before? Have you ever lied or sworn falsely in all your life? Have you ever been drunk or over-eaten before? Have you ever taken what was not yours or ever coveted your friend's goods before? If the answer to any of them is 'No', take a look at the following.

The list goes like this: wickedness, malice; envy, murder, strife, deception, evil-mindedness, backbiting, hating God, violence, pride, boasting, inventing of evil things, disobeying parents.

If you have ever done any of these things more than once and have never effectively dealt with it, this may be your area of weakness. It is very likely the devil will continue to tempt you in those areas until they are adequately dealt with.

There is another concern I would like to explore. There are people who know the areas of their weaknesses, but deny the ability of the devil to tempt them in those areas. This can be seen as pride or arrogance. No one is ever too big or too spiritual to be tempted of the devil. The devil tempted our Lord and Saviour Jesus, and he is not a respecter of persons.

"Therefore let him who thinks he stands take heed lest he fall" (1 Corinthians 10:12).

"Brethren, if a man is overtaken in any trespass, you who are spiritual restore such a one in a spirit of gentleness, considering yourself lest you also be tempted" (Galatians 6:1).

Knowing your weaknesses will help to avoid being tempted.

Recognise the triggers and avoid them

Let us take a quick look at some simple steps that can be taken so as to avoid being tempted.

- If your weakness is gluttony, avoid frequenting the kitchen or taking a job in a fast food restaurant or working as a kitchen porter.

- If it is lust, avoid passing by the porn magazines at supermarkets. Adopt a different route.

- It may not be wise to take up a job as a bartender if you are struggling with alcohol neither would you do yourself any favours in taking up a job at a night club if you cannot handle lust.

- I counsel that, if you are dealing with lust, you should not visit a new Christian (of the opposite sex) alone even in an emergency.

- I would also counsel that you should not volunteer to be an Usher or Treasurer for any organisation (including the Church) if you are struggling with stealing since you may have to handle money.

- If you are an impulse or emotional buyer, avoid window shopping.

Be watchful

Three times in the Gospels, the Bible admonished us to pray not to enter into temptation.

"Watch and pray, lest you enter into temptation. The spirit indeed is willing, but the flesh is weak" (Matthew 26:41).

"Watch and pray, lest you enter into temptation. The spirit indeed is willing, but the flesh is weak" (Mark 14:38).

"When He came to the place, He said to them, "Pray that you may not enter into temptation" (Luke 22:40).

Praying against temptation is to be done daily. It is part of what has been described as the Lord's Prayer. As we commit every other activity of the day into God's hands, we also need to pray against being tempted.

"Give us this day our daily bread. And forgive us our debts, as we forgive our debtors. And do not lead us into temptation, but deliver us from the evil one. For Yours is the kingdom and the power and the glory forever. Amen" (Matthew 6:11-13).

We pray daily for bread. However, that is not to be done exclusively. As we pray for our daily bread, we also need to pray daily, *'Lead me not into temptation.'*

Why do we need to watch? Jesus answered,

"The spirit indeed is willing, but the flesh is weak" (Matthew 26:41).

Temptation is a struggle between the spirit and the flesh. When we pray, we communicate with our spirits but by watching, we communicate with our flesh so we can effectively deal with the inner struggle. Believe me, our flesh are weak. We need to be more discerning and not appear too spiritual. Even when we have prayed, we do not ignore the feelings, but keep watching.

Watching and praying are to be done together. One is not above the other. Some of us just pray but we do not watch. When you pray not to be tempted, you have to keep the eyes open. You cannot claim victory on the axle of prayer alone. You need to watch continually for the telltale signs of temptation. Moreover, when you see them, do not just recount or recite the scriptures or start praying, expecting they will go away. Do something.

Let me use an example. When you are watching a movie alone in the comfort of your home, hold the remote control close by. If something strange appears on your screen (as they sometimes do), do not start to pray, just change the channel. No amount of praying will change the programme. This is not the time to 'watch and pray.' Let your fingers do the watching and praying, change the dial.

On the other hand, when you are counselling the opposite sex alone or conducting a deliverance session, have someone close by and do not lock the doors. Invite a mentee or you can ask your spouse to join you. Even after you have taken all precautions, keep your eyes wide open as you pray. Watch and pray. If you are ministering to a lady and suddenly the lady's shoulder strap should loosen (as they sometimes do), you will immediately notice and you can run just as Joseph did.

Keep your heart pure

The mind is in the realm of the soul. It is the seat of intellect and will. It is where the fiercest battles take place – a place the devil wants to control. So the devil may suggest things into the mind (also known as the heart, from the Hebrew word '*leb*'). If you allow him to win you over in the area of your thinking, you will carry out his instructions.

"Above all else, guard your heart, for it affects everything you do" (Proverbs 4:23, NLT).

At the instance of Jesus' temptations, the devil may not have appeared to Him physically. He may have only suggested a few things to His heart, but Jesus was discerning enough to recognise the plot of the evil one.

The Little Sisters of the Poor were going from door to door in a French city, soliciting alms for old people. One nun called at the house of a rich free-thinker who said he would give 1000 francs if she would have a glass of champagne with him. It was an embarrassing situation for the nun, and she hesitated. However, the hesitation was short – after all, 1000 francs meant many loaves of bread. A servant brought the bottle and poured, and the brave little nun emptied the glass. And then she said, "And now, sir, another glass please, at the same price." She got it. And the devil got her[1].

The devil still deploys the same strategies today. He wants to steal your heart, but you should not let him in. You should bring every evil thought into captivity to the obedience of Christ.

"For though we walk in the flesh, we do not war according to the flesh. For the weapons of our warfare are not carnal but mighty in God for pulling down strongholds, casting down arguments and every high thing that exalts itself against the knowledge of God, bringing every

thought into captivity to the obedience of Christ, and being ready to punish all disobedience when your obedience is fulfilled" (2 Corinthians 10:3-6).

When the devil suggests something contrary to the will of God, immediately replace it with God's words. That way, your actions will be godly. This should save you, but if you do not, you will eventually carry out what those thoughts.

"Don't copy the behaviour and customs of this world, but let God transform you into a new person by changing the way you think. Then you will know what God wants you to do, and you will know how good and pleasing and perfect His will really is" (Romans 12:1-2, NLT).

"Finally, brethren, whatever things are true, whatever things are noble, whatever things are just, whatever things are pure, whatever things are lovely, whatever things are of good report, if there is any virtue and if there is anything praiseworthy – meditate on these things" (Philippians 4:8).

Draw near to God

The second step in temptation is being drawn away. Before the enemy is ever going to succeed in destroying you, he will of necessity have to drag you away from God. As long as you are close to God in your heart, and your actions, he can never succeed in overcoming you. That is not to say that he will not try, but he will never win you over. The devil is after your mind. Let me give you a simple principle: *'The closer you are to God, the farther away you are from the devil.'* The converse also holds true: *'The farther away you are from God, the closer you are to the devil.'* So you can conclude: if you want to be far away from the devil, draw near to God.

> *"So humble yourselves before God. Resist the Devil, and he will flee from you. Draw close to God, and God will draw close to you. Wash your hands, you sinners; purify your hearts, you hypocrites" (James 4:7-8, NLT).*

The scriptures tell us that we may be drawn away from the simplicity and purity of devotion to Christ. The Gospel is so simple people walk away from it. If our love for God or the things of God is second place, something is wrong, and we need to be careful and return to God.

> *"But I am afraid lest somehow, as the serpent deceived Eve by his craftiness, your minds may be led astray from the simplicity and purity of devotion to Christ" (2 Corinthians 11:3, LEB).*

Enduring Temptation

John Paton was a missionary in the New Hebrides Islands. One night hostile natives surrounded the mission station, intent on burning out the Patons and killing them. Paton and his wife prayed during that terror-filled night that God would deliver them. When daylight came, they were amazed to see their attackers leave. A year later, the chief of the tribe was converted to Christ. Remembering what had happened, Paton asked the chief what had kept him from burning down the house and killing them. The chief replied in surprise, "Who were all those men with you there?" Paton knew no men were present – but the chief said he was afraid to attack because he had seen hundreds of big men in shining garments with drawn swords circling the mission station[2].

There are instances where you've done all there is to do but the objects, that bring temptation, are immovable. What more can you do? Endure.

"No temptation has overtaken you except such as is common to man, but God is faithful, Who will not allow you to be tempted beyond what you are able, but with the temptation will also make a way of escape, that you may be able to bear it" (1 Corinthians 10:13).

Sometimes it may be possible to run or walk away from certain types of temptation. There are others however with which you may not find things easy if you decide to run. Running or walking away would appear as if you are walking away from self. I'll give an example.

If you trained as a chef and have built a career as a chef, how would you deal with gluttony? Walk away from your profession? No, you just endure and bear it.

How about this? If you are struggling with pornography, you have a lot to bear. They come at you from all angles; from the television to the billboards; from the public phone booths to the Internet. They are everywhere. If someone suddenly decides to build a clubhouse near your house, you can relocate. If you go to the shopping mall and you find porn magazines on the shelves, you can walk away. You have a choice to visit the beach or not to. However, there is nothing you can do when summer arrives, and people wear suggestive clothing. Are you going to hide during the summer and only come out in winter? No, you just have to endure and bear it.

That was why Apostle Paul said '*that you may be able to bear it.*' Temptation places on you a heavy burden. It is like being under a weight. Though it is not physical, it can indeed be heavy. The Greek word translated bear is *hupophero*. It means to 'bear from underneath.' It means to carry a load and to endure. So you see, "*you may be able to bear it.*"

Moreover, you can take it to Jesus. He is your burden-bearer. Whatever you cannot do for yourself, He can do for you. He said in his word,

> "*Come to Me, all you who labour and are heavy laden, and I will give you rest. Take My yoke upon you and learn from Me, for I am gentle and lowly in heart, and you will find rest for your souls. For My yoke is easy and My burden is light*" (Matthew 11:28-30).

There is a reward when we endure temptation. There is a crown when we persevere. Enduring temptation is a way of demonstrating our love for God. When we fall because of temptation, we sin against ourselves, others and God. The stories of Joseph and David clearly show this to be true. Joseph said this when he was chased by his master's wife,

> "*No one here has more authority than I do! He has held back nothing from me except you, because you are his wife. How could I ever do such a wicked thing? It would be a great sin against God*" (Genesis 39:9, NLT).

David also echoed this revelation after his marital affair with Bathsheba,

"Against You, and You alone, have I sinned; I have done what is evil in your sight..." *(Psalms 51:4a, NLT).*

The crown of life is God's way of rewarding the endurance.

"Blessed is the man who endures temptation for when he has been approved, he will receive the crown of life which the Lord has promised to those who love Him" *(James 1:12).*

Key Points to Remember

- Recognise and identify your areas of weaknesses. It is dangerous not to be aware of your areas of weaknesses or deny they exist. Help yourself, get help.
- Recognise what triggers your weakness and avoid them. After you have identified the weakness, stay away from what may trigger it.
- Be Watchful. You need to watch continually for the tell-tale signs of temptation. Moreover, when you see them, do not just recount or recite the scriptures or start praying, expecting they will go away. Do something.

- When the devil suggests something to your heart that contradicts the will of God, immediately replace it with God's words. This should save you from carrying out evil thoughts. This way, your actions will be godly.
- Stay close to God. As long as you are close to God in your heart, and your actions, he can never succeed in overcoming you. That is not to say that he will not try, but he will never win you over.
- Where it may not be easy to walk away from temptation, you may have to endure with God's help. There are instances where you've done all there is to do but the objects, that bring temptation, are immovable. Just endure, and you will be rewarded.

[1]*Bits & Pieces*, April 4, 1991.

[2]*Today in the Word*, MBI, October, 1991, p. 18.

Chapter Nine

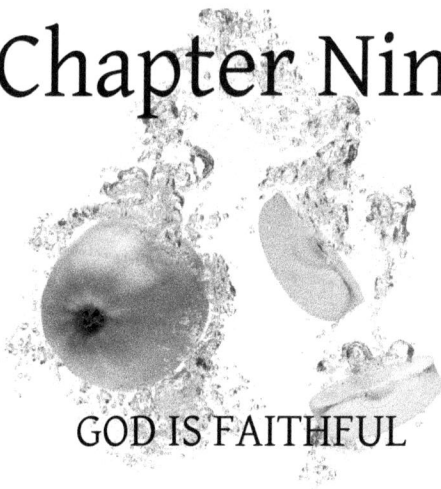

GOD IS FAITHFUL

Chapter Nine

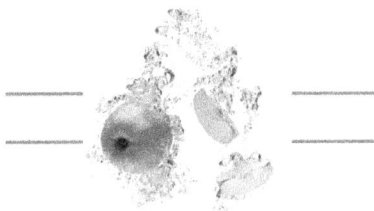

GOD IS FAITHFUL

Let us now look at the faithfulness of God during our times of struggle.

"No temptation has overtaken you except such as is common to man, but God is faithful, Who will not allow you to be tempted beyond what you are able, but with the temptation will also make a way of escape, that you may be able to bear it" (1 Corinthians 10:13).

Your Temptation is Common

Whatever it is you are going through is not unusual. Because of the depth of our pain, many of us would like to think that our situation is peculiar and relish such uniqueness. We even ignore people's concern for our welfare because we feel they do not understand our struggles. Whatever name you call it, however you describe it, it is common. Your temptation is not unique. What you are experiencing has happened to someone in the past; it is happening to someone right now, and it will still happen to someone in the not too distant future.

> *"Be alert, be on the watch! Your enemy, the Devil, roams round like a roaring lion, looking for someone to devour. Be firm in your faith and resist him, because you know that your fellow-believers in all the world are going through the same kind of sufferings" (1 Peter 5:8-9, GNB).*

> *"History merely repeats itself. It has all been done before. Nothing under the sun is truly new" (Ecclesiastes 1:9, NLT).*

God Is Faithful

Secondly, God is faithful. God knows what you are going through, and He also knows about it. You may think God has deserted you because your circumstance remains unchanged, or there is no help from Him. He knows. He is just watching how you are handling things.

> *"And the LORD said: 'I have surely seen the oppression of My people who are in Egypt, and have heard their cry because of their taskmasters, for I know their sorrows" (Exodus 3:7).*

God is faithful. He will not allow you to be tempted beyond your ability. He has deposited on the inside of you the ability to withstand whatever He has allowed the Devil to throw at you. You cannot fail.

> *"Dearest friends, you were always so careful to follow my instructions when I was with you. And now that I am away you must be even more careful to put into action God's saving work in your lives, obeying God with deep reverence and fear. For God is working in you, giving you the desire to obey Him and the power to do what pleases Him" (Philippians 2:12-13, NLT).*

Even when we fail or falter, that will not change God's personality.

> *"If we are faithless, He remains faithful; for He cannot deny Himself" (2 Timothy 2:13, NLT).*

God Allowed It

Thirdly, whatever you are going through is permitted. God allowed it. You are tempted with permission. God would never tempt you. It is Satan's job to tempt you, and he cannot tempt you until he has God's permission.

"...Who (God) will not allow you to be tempted beyond what you are able" (1 Corinthians 10:13).

Did you notice the word 'allow?' If you are facing any challenges now, it is because God allowed it.

Satan is a vagabond. After first assigning responsibilities to members of his team, Satan just walks about looking for scapegoats to destroy. Moreover, the Bible says the devil walks around *'seeking whom he may devour.'* The Bible did not say he devours anyone he seeks; only seeks those whom he may devour, perhaps he will find one.

"Be sober, be vigilant; because your adversary the devil walks about like a roaring lion, seeking whom he may devour" (1 Peter 5:8).

"Now there was a day when the sons of God came to present themselves before the LORD, and Satan also came among them. And the LORD said to Satan, 'From where do you

come?' So Satan answered the LORD and said, 'From going to and from on the earth, and from walking back and forth on it.' Then the LORD said to Satan, 'Have you considered My servant Job, that there is none like him on the earth, a blameless and upright man, one who fears God and shuns evil?' So Satan answered the LORD and said, 'Does Job fear God for nothing? Have You not made a hedge around him, around his household, and around all that he has on every side? You have blessed the work of his hands, and his possessions have increased in the land. But now, stretch out Your hand and touch all that he has, and he will surely curse You to Your face!' And the LORD said to Satan, 'Behold, all that he has is in your power; only do not lay a hand on his person.' So Satan went out from the presence of the LORD" (Job 1:6-12).*

There Is a Limit

Fourthly, there is a limit, a cap on your suffering. Let me remind you again what that scripture says.

"Who (God) will not allow you to be tempted beyond what you are able" (1 Corinthians 10:13).

"'Behold, all that he has is in your power; only do not lay a hand on his person.' So Satan went out from the presence of the LORD" (Job 1:12).

God has put a cap on your sufferings based on the grace of endurance you have been given. Again I say to you; you can handle it. Concerning Job, God told Satan, "There is a boundary you must never cross." Satan said, 'Yes Sir,' then left.

God will not allow you to be tempted beyond what you are able. That means you have the ability. Even if you doubt yourself, God can trust you. Your temptation has a limit. It will not go beyond a certain limit – your ability. No temptation can be overpowering. So make sure you do not fall.

There Is A Way of Escape

Finally, there is a way of escape. To be perfectly honest, God will always provide an escape route when the challenges seem overwhelming and overpowering. The problem with many of us is that we are so caught up in our afflictions to the point we have been blinded to the many escape routes God provides.

Look for the exit sign; there is always one. There are situations you do not need to pray or even ask questions. Three times in the scriptures we are admonished to take to our heels against the temptation of immorality, love of money, and lust.

"Flee immorality. Every other sin that a man commits is outside the body, but the immoral man sins against his own body" (1 Corinthians 6:18, NASB).

"But flee from these things you man of God and pursue righteousness, godliness, faith, love, perseverance and gentleness" (1 Timothy 6:11, NASB).

We are admonished to flee from youthful lust.

"Run from anything that stimulates youthful lust. Follow anything that makes you want to do right. Pursue faith and love and peace, and enjoy the companionship of those who call on the Lord with pure hearts" (2 Timothy 2:22, NLT).

Key Points to Remember

- Trust in God's faithfulness. He has deposited on the inside of you the ability to withstand whatever He has allowed the Devil to throw at you. You cannot fail.
- Don't blame God. Whatever you are going through is permitted. God allowed it. You are tempted with permission. God

would never tempt you. If you are facing any challenges now, it is because God allowed it.

- Present Satan no place in your life. He can only occupy the space that we allow him. The Bible did not say he devours anyone he seeks; only seeks whom he may devour, perhaps he will find one.

- Your temptation has a limit. It will not go beyond a certain limit—your ability. No temptation can be overpowering. If you fall, it is not God's fault.

- Look for the exit sign, there is always one. There are situations you do not need to pray or even ask questions.

Other books by Sam O. Adewunmi

GOOD FINISH TO BAD START

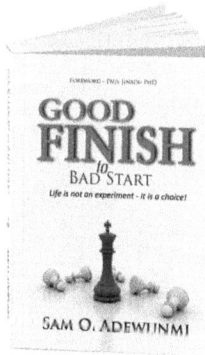

Life is about choices. You are a product of the choices you made yesterday. What you will become tomorrow will be determined by the choices you are making right now.

In this captivating book, Pastor Sam shares profound insights on areas of your life where choices that affect your future are made. In simple practical steps, he shows how by the help of God, you can go from a poor start to a good finish.

Your past may not be your fault but what you become tomorrow is your responsibility, and... your choice!

ISBN 978-1-907734-44-1

YOUR BASKET, KNEADING BOWL AND BARN

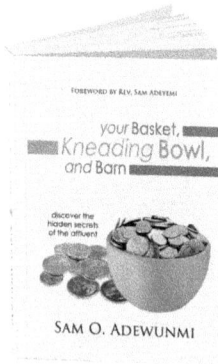

"I have observed how people picked themselves up from
unthinkable depths of lack and rose to become the most successful
people of our time. Walk with me and I will show you how."
Author.

You may be born into poverty, but you are not created to be
poor, and you do not have to die a pauper. Most Christians are not
aware that the Bible addresses a wealth of economic issues of
stewardship, thrift and financial empowerment.

'Your Basket, Kneading Bowl and Barn' is a solid, concise mix of
biblical insight, biblical wisdom, and common sense. It exposes the
reader to current World Financial System threatening true financial
freedom, how to avoid its trickery, become financially independent,
and live the life of abundance God promised.

Take hold of the principles in this book, and you too will become
a living testimony that it is possible to prosper, experience financial
freedom, and to break free from the curse of poverty. After all,
poverty is a choice! Since God did not force salvation on you, which
happens to be His greater desire, He will not force you to be rich.

ISBN 978-1-907734-14-4